Days in the life

The Lost Beatles Archives

STAR PUBLISHING
2 Lansdowne Row
London, England WIX 8HL

Edited by R.E. Robinson
Written by Richard Buskin
Designed by Ben Mallalieu
Repro by Ripping Image
Printed in South Korea

EVERY now and then something magical happens. It may not be all that often, but it happens just frequently enough to remind you that there really are some miracles left in this workaday world. This book comes about as a result of one of these miracles.

"There's been a discovery!" It was a typical, dreary London day in January, 1998 when this electrifying news was delivered to me by telephone. It's a moment that I'll never, ever forget. A fellow who lived just outside London had been cleaning out some of his late father's belongings when he had made an incredible find. There, in a small metal box in a corner of the attic was an assortment of undeveloped film, taken in the mid-1960s. This film had been taken by his father, who had worked as a freelance photographer some 30 years ago. Wonderfully, miraculously, this film contained some amazing and historic shots of The Beatles . . . shots which have never been seen before. This was truly a once-in-a-lifetime discovery, a gift for the entire world.

The Beatles mean different things to different people, but no matter who you are The Beatles have touched your life in some way. Never before, and I dare say never again will there be a musical group that will change the world in the way that >

3

< John, Paul, George and Ringo have done so effortlessly. Their music lives inside all of us, and we'll carry it with us for our entire lives.

Thinking back to those wonderful and thrilling days in 1963 when I first became aware of the phenomenon known as "The Beatles," I still get chills up and down my spine. What special times those were as the Fab Four exploded onto the scene, sweeping all of us up in a cloud of optimism, awe and excitement.

The photos that you are about to see are from those years; those impossibly young and turbulent years when the whole world stopped whatever it was doing to turn an inquisitive ear to the most thrilling and emotional popular music that this world has ever heard.

So, take a deep breath and get ready. When you turn this page you are going to become a participant in the wonderful history of the most influential and exciting musical group that the world has ever known.

I hope you enjoy these photos as much as we have enjoyed bringing them to you.

With very best wishes,

R E Robinson
London, September 1998

4

DAYS IN THE LIFE
THE LOST BEATLES ARCHIVES

"FOUR Frenzied Little Lord Fauntleroys Who Are Earning £5,000 A Week," is how Britain's *Daily Mirror* newspaper described The Beatles in 1963, and here are the young men who were at the center of the storm during that landmark year. Ringo, John, Paul and George sport the 'moptop' hairdos that they had been introduced to by photographer-friend Astrid Kirchherr in Hamburg, Germany, together with the sharp suit-shirt-tie look that bore the influence of their manager, Brian Epstein.

Captured at a photo call in between recording sessions and concert dates around Britain, the Fab Four, as they were quickly dubbed, have clearly had some of the rough edges knocked off during their transition from the leather-clad, greasy-haired rockers of just a couple of years before. Incidentally, on November 2, 1963 a *Mirror* headline would coin the phrase 'Beatlemania' in an article focussing on the teen frenzy that was sweeping the nation.

THE fans were quick to learn their Liverpudlian idols' vital stats:

John Winston Lennon
Born: October 9, 1940
Hair: Brown
Eyes: Brown
Height: 5'11"
Main instruments: Rhythm guitar, harmonica, keyboards

James Paul McCartney (Paul McCartney)
Born: June 18, 1942
Hair: Black
Eyes: Hazel
Height: 5'11"
Main instruments: Bass guitar, keyboards

George Harrison
Born: February 25, 1943
Hair: Brown
Eyes: Dark brown
Height: 5'11"
Main instruments: Lead guitar

Richard Starkey a.k.a. Ringo Starr
Born: July 7, 1940
Hair: Dark Brown
Eyes: Blue
Height: 5'8"
Main instruments: drums, percussion

ASIDE from their hairstyles, The Beatles started a number of trends during their first year of nationwide fame in Britain. To start with there were the Pierre Cardin collarless jackets which they wore from April to October of 1963, and which would spark a worldwide craze even though the group never actually sported them once they arrived in the States in early 1964. By that time they were wearing more conventional suits as designed by their personal tailor, Douglas Millings.

John would later assert that he and George initially tried to resist Brian Epstein's efforts to sharpen the band's image, but that Paul had supported their managers' wishes. Paul, on the other hand, has since challenged this statement, insisting that his colleagues were more than happy to go along with any idea that might help secure their success.

IN terms of image, another way in which The Beatles immediately set themselves apart from other clean-cut pop idols of the early Sixties was the manner in which they made no effort to disguise the fact that they all smoked, and that — shock, horror — they also enjoyed mixing Scotch with their Coca-Cola.

Today such stark, brutal 'admissions' would be laughable, but even back then they must have prompted amusement among those people who had, only a short while before, seen 'the boys' drinking on stage in Liverpool and popping pills in Hamburg.

TIME for some lighthearted chat during this 1963 photo call. In the earliest years of their success The Beatles were apparently willing to pose in front of as many photographers' lenses as possible, but of course as time wore on and their need for publicity declined such photo opportunities became scarcer. Eventually the only pictures that they officially posed for were those taken by photographers who they themselves actually commissioned.

Among the people who assumed this role between 1962 and 1969 were Dezo Hoffmann, Angus McBean, Richard Avedon, Cyrus Andrews, Robert Freeman, John Launois, Philip Gotlop, Robert Whitaker, Oluf Nissen, Don McCullin, Tony Bramwell, Stephen Goldblatt, Iain Macmillan and Ethan Russell.

Tut,

tut! Don't put your feet up on the coffee table! Well, this may not have been the right kind of example to set to their younger fans, but at least it afforded The Beatles the opportunity to show off their well-worn Cuban-heeled boots, another of the fashion accessories with which they were closely associated in 1963 and 1964.

As you can see, even though Paul's pants and Ringo's light-colored suit helped mix things up a little at public appearances such as this, the basic idea was for the band to conform to a uniform image. Only once they had stopped touring in 1966 would Messrs. Lennon, McCartney, Harrison and Starr begin to dress like the individuals that they truly were.

WHAT to do while waiting around in a sparsely furnished dressing room prior to a concert in one of the many theaters and cinemas up and down Britain? How about a quick game of cards? While Ringo and George are clearly up to no good, John is apparently quite happy to show his hand to Paul.

Captured during their November 1–December 13, 1963 'Autumn Tour' of the UK, The Beatles were earning £300 a night to perform the same half-hour set each time, comprising 'I Saw Her Standing There', 'From Me To You', 'All My Loving', 'You Really Got A Hold On Me', 'Roll Over Beethoven', 'Boys', 'Till There Was You', 'She Loves You', 'Money (That's What I Want)' and 'Twist And Shout'.

TIME for a ciggie. Among the many trivia details that were circulated by The Beatles' publicity machine during the early 1960's was the apparent fact that they smoked Lark cigarettes, an American brand that consequently enjoyed increased popularity on both sides of the Atlantic. Still, this did little to bridge the language gap between Britain and the United States, whereby a Brit who is proposing to smoke could find himself being somewhat misunderstood if asking an American if he "fancies a fag".

THE Beatles' Autumn Tour was the band's fourth jaunt around Britain during the breathless year of 1963. The first, running from February 2 to March 3, saw John, Paul, George and Ringo performing bottom on a six-act bill headed by 16-year-old London vocalist, Helen Shapiro. By the end of that stint The Beatles were closing the first half of the show, and just six days later they set off on their second nationwide package tour. Lasting until March 9, this experienced a change in billing on the very first night, The Beatles taking over the top spot from two Americans who were supposed to share it, Chris Montez and Tommy Roe.

The Fab Four's popularity was snowballing at a rapid rate, and the next American celebrity to sample this first-hand was Roy Orbison, who was usurped by them as the headlining act during their May 18–June 9 tour of Britain. Never again would The Beatles play second fiddle to anyone.

THE time: November 4, 1963. The place: London's Prince of Wales Theatre. The occasion: The Royal Command Performance, in the presence of Her Royal Highness The Queen Mother and Princess Margaret. An annual, up-market variety show, this featured The Beatles appearing seventh on a 19-act bill that included Marlene Dietrich, Buddy Greco, Harry Secombe, Tommy Steele and a pair of popular puppet pigs named Pinky and Perky.

Here Ringo, standing beside comedian Eric Sykes, watches George converse with Princess Margaret's husband, Lord Snowdon, during the obligatory VIP meet 'n' greet session. As for the show itself, The Beatles performed 'From Me To You', 'She Loves You' and 'Till There Was You', before John invited audience participation for 'Twist And Shout' by suggesting, "Would the people in the cheaper seats clap your hands, and the rest of you, if you'll just rattle your jewelry."

24

A British bobby prevents a teenager from prising open some iron bars with her bare hands as she attempts to gain access to The Beatles' dressing room, following one of the gigs on the group's 1963 'Autumn Tour'. The police, however, weren't always so successful.

In Carlisle during the previous tour, around 600 rabid fans waited in line for 36 hours before the box office opened, yet, when it did, their hysteria resulted in some of them being projected through store windows and nine being rushed to the hospital. A short time later, in Newcastle-upon-Tyne, a reported 10,000 Beatlemaniacs "went wild in a fantastic stampede" while waiting to buy tickets according to *The Daily Mirror*. More than 120 teens had to receive first aid, seven were treated for shock and one girl had to cover herself with a blanket while handing over her money, having somehow lost her jeans amid all of the fuss.

"**IF** it won't go, blow!" appears to be George's philosophy as he and his three colleagues stare intently at a pair of toy racing cars. This, unfortunately, was the kind of lame pose that was requested of The Beatles during the early years of their fame, tying in with their publicity image as a bunch of healthy, happy-go-lucky, fun-loving youngsters who spent most of their time smiling for no apparent reason.

The reality, of course, was far removed from the myth, and it doesn't take too much imagination to guess what 'the boys' were probably muttering immediately after this shot was taken.

28

DECEMBER 2, 1963:

Paul and George go over their lines while Eric Morecambe, complete with Beatles wig, shares a joke with Ringo and John during rehearsals and taping for ATV's *The Morecambe And Wise Show*, which was broadcast across Britain on April 18, 1964.

After the Liverpudlian pop sensations had performed 'This Boy', 'All My Loving' and 'I Want To Hold Your Hand', they were joined by Eric and his comic partner Ernie Wise for a scripted 'ad-lib' routine in which Morecambe addressed John, Paul and George as "The Kaye Sisters" (a British female singing trio), and Ringo as "Bongo". Lennon, McCartney, Harrison and Wise then 'decided' to don straw hats and striped jackets for a rendition of the old Alice Fay/Doris Day hit, 'Moonlight Bay', but while Ringo drummed sedately in the background Morecambe entered the proceedings in his wig and collarless jacket, dancing like a lunatic and shouting, "yeah, yeah, yeah," "twist and shout" and, in 'mistaken' reference to Gerry and the Pacemakers, "I like it".

U NTIL Eric's death in 1984 Morecambe and Wise were among Britain's most beloved comedians, and in 1994 Paul McCartney named The Beatles' appearance on their show as his favorite out of all of the group's television performances.

Here they pose with Ernie around one of the Associated TeleVision cameras, having already had their Royal Command Show performance broadcast across the nation by the same network on November 10, 1963.

PAUL McCartney, Hofner 'violin' bass guitar in hand, is captured backstage at ATV's Elstree Studio Centre in Borehamwood, Hertfordshire during taping of *The Morecambe And Wise Show*. The photographer at far left is famed celebrity lensman, Dezo Hoffmann.

A Hungarian emigré, Hoffmann took many of The Beatles' early publicity shots, including the first ones of them working at EMI's recording studios in Abbey Road (on September 4, 1962) and the widely-seen 1963 poses of the Fab Four in their collarless jackets. He followed the band when they visited France and the United States in 1964, but a falling-out with John Lennon basically ended the professional friendship.

Dressing Rooms
Nos 9-17 & 28-38

As Paul and George look on, Eric Morecambe tries to enhance Ringo's own moptop with a Beatles Wig. Ringo needn't have worried; the wig was made to "fit all head sizes".

Manufactured in Britain by the Bell Toy Company and bearing the slogan 'Be With It, Wear a Beatles Wig', no less than half a ton of these items were shipped to the States in February of 1964 in order to try and meet the skyrocketing demand for all things Fab. At that point the Americans came up with "the only authentic" version, courtesy of Lowell Toy Manufacturing, which was subsequently produced in such large quantities that today a sample is worth only about a fifth of the price paid by collectors for its rarer British counterpart.

ALL dressed up and, er, loving it. Well, at least Paul looks fairly happy, while George is still undecided. As for John and Ringo . . .

The Beatles' appearance on *The Morecambe And Wise Show* may have been a high point in their TV career, but clearly even the novelty of wearing straw hats and striped jackets wore off after a while.

LOOKING pensive yet innocent in this photo taken in early 1964, Paul McCartney was always the Beatle with the greatest drive and ambition. Adept at playing any number of instruments, including the drums and lead guitar in addition to keyboards and his own bass, 'Macca' would often help to direct affairs inside the recording studio, instructing his fellow band members on what parts they should play.

At the same time he was also the Beatle who most enjoyed touring and, after the group had quit the road, kept coming up with new artistic ideas and business ventures in order to sustain his colleagues' interest and keep the unit together. Ultimately, however, this same level of intensity would alienate John, George and Ringo, and help contribute towards the band's acrimonious demise.

"NOTHING to declare!" For reasons best known to their then-publicity man, Brian Sommerville, George, John and Paul give a French customs official a friendly salute on their arrival at Le Bourget in Paris on January 14, 1964. Ringo, stranded in a fogbound Liverpool while visiting his parents, was not nearly so happy. He and road manager Neil Aspinall would have to take an 8 a.m. flight via London the next day, just hours before The Beatles were due to perform their first concert on French soil, at the Cinéma Cyrano in Versailles.

A grand total of 60 French teenagers had turned out to greet Lennon, McCartney and Harrison on their airport arrival. As things turned out, this would prove to be an ominous sign of the events that were to follow.

GEORGE grapples with a cheese sandwich while on a visit to the Eiffel Tower, during The Beatles' three-week engagement at the Olympia Theatre in Paris from January 16 to February 4, 1964. Performing on a nine-act bill that included French vocalist Sylvie Vartan and Texas-born singer Trini Lopez, The Beatles were somewhat underwhelmed by the lack of audience enthusiasm at each of the shows, and perhaps disappointed to find that they could walk down Paris' main boulevard, Les Champs Elysées, without being accosted by fans. The same could hardly be said elsewhere.

It was during the Paris residency that the group learned that 'I Want To Hold Your Hand' had shot to the top of the Cash Box singles chart in America. So much for the popular evening newspaper, France-Soir, dismissing Les Beatles as "delinquents" and "has-beens". Vive la difference!

A moment of quiet reflection during a less than ideal Parisian visit as George sits alone at the Eiffel Tower. On The Beatles' opening night at the Olympia Theatre he openly complained of sabotage after the band's amplification equipment broke down three times during the performance. Before the show punches had been thrown when press officer Brian Somerville had tried to keep reporters and photographers out of the group's dressing room. After the show the famous Paris department store, Les Galeries Lafayette, decided to cancel its plans to fill one of its main windows with Beatles merchandise. The Anglo-French friction was tangible.

The Beatles played two and sometimes three shows a day during the three-week engagement, with just a couple of days off in between. On the second of these both George and John flew back to London for a few hours' respite.

DEREK and George. The Beatles' lead guitarist and Derek Taylor, the Northern show-business correspondent for national newspaper The Daily Express, became firm friends after Taylor was hired by Brian Epstein to be his personal assistant, and their friendship would last right up until Taylor's death in 1997.

Derek first saw The Beatles at the Manchester Odeon on May 30, 1963, and within months he was ghost-writing a weekly column by George in the Express. In 1964 he ghosted Epstein's autobiography, *A Cellarful of Noise*, and when The Beatles parted the ways with press officer Brian Sommerville that same year Taylor stepped into his shoes. Later he would act in the same capacity for The Beach Boys, The Byrds and Captain Beefheart, and co-found the Monterey International Pop Festival in 1967 before returning to The Fabs' fold the following year as press officer for their own Apple Records label.

During the 1970's Derek rose to Vice President at Warner Brothers Records in America, and then left the company in 1978 to write and consult on numerous books, including his own autobiographies and that of George, entitled *I Me Mine*.

AN autograph opportunity for a young French fan. The Beatles signed literally thousands of items down the years, from records and photos to concert programs and paper napkins, yet there were also plenty of other 'official' autographs that were less than authentic.

Due to the huge demand for all things Fab during the mid-Sixties, and with The Beatles' blessing, several of the band's assistants became adept at copying the signatures of John, Paul, George and Ringo, so that during plane trips they could churn out 'autographed' publicity pics by the bucket-load. Consequently, unless people now have items that they personally saw one or more of The Beatles signing, it is often difficult to tell the difference between the bogus version and the real thing.

"**L**OOKIT, I thought I was supposed to be getting a change of scenery, and so far I've been in a train and a room, and a car and a room, and a room and a room," says Wilfred Brambell, portraying Paul's grandfather in The Beatles' first film, *A Hard Day's Night*.

This, however, was a fact of life for the Fab Four by 1964, when they usually had to be smuggled in and out of concert theaters and hotels in the back of police vans and even armored cars in order to escape the marauding teenage fans. Paul, John and Ringo still manage to raise smiles for this photo taken early during that hectic year, but George's expression really sums up how they would all soon be feeling about this mind-numbing routine.

In the meantime, John has taken to wearing a peaked cap and dark glasses by way of tribute to the look of his new hero, American folk singer Bob Dylan.

MORE

of the same, except that this time around The Beatles are purposely trapped inside a train during location filming for *A Hard Day's Night*. Between March 2-6, 1964 they shot the scenes that took place on the train as it traveled from London's Paddington Station to various destinations in England's West Country, yet in order to avoid the fans they would embark each day at Acton Main Line in West London and then jump off either there or at other stops such as West Ealing, Westbourne Park and Hayes & Harlington. Then they would travel home in their chauffeur-driven limousine.

Meanwhile, the film's opening scene, in which the band members are chased along the station platform by marauding teenagers, was shot at London's Marylebone Station on April 5 and 12.

THE world's four most famous hairstyles are tended to by a quartet of extras on the set of *A Hard Day's Night*, yet one of these 'schoolgirls' would soon loom large in The Beatles' legend. The pretty blonde at far left applying the tender touch to George is Patricia Ann Boyd, a 20-year-old model who had previously worked with director Richard Lester on a television ad for Smith's Crisps.

Although Paul briefly chats her up in the film, in real life it was George who took an instant shining to Pattie. Already engaged, she initially rejected his advances, but there was no way that she could resist a Beatle for long and on January 21, 1966 the two of them would marry. Thereafter Pattie would introduce George to Transcendental Meditation, only to subsequently feel alienated when he dedicated more and more of his time to the pursuit of spiritual enlightenment. Embarking on an affair with George's friend, guitarist Eric Clapton, Pattie would divorce the ex-Beatle in 1974 and later undertake a short-lived marriage to the blues virtuoso.

"VOT eez goin' on here?" Looking a little the worse for wear after some sleepless nights, George hams it up on the set of *A Hard Day's Night*.

Although having only recently turned 21, the youngest member of The Beatles always displayed a strong character, and during the making of the band's first film he ensured that scriptwriter Alun Owen and director Dick Lester gave him an equivalent amount of screen time to that of his three colleagues. Each had a solo scene: John being recognized by a female production assistant in a corridor at the Scala Theatre; Paul flirting with an actress who is rehearsing in period costume; George being mistakenly auditioned as a male model by a TV director; and Ringo wandering alone through London and by the banks of the River Thames. George, however, wanted to be featured some more, and so Alun Owen wrote in the segment where he gives the band's assistant, Shake, a pretend-shave in the mirror.

As it happens, it was Paul who would end up being short-changed. His solo scene was cut from the finished picture.

LENNON subtly eyes up actress Julia Foster on the set of *A Hard Day's Night* . . .

...THEN he makes his move.

MARCH 31, 1964: George tries to teach Ringo a guitar chord or two while waiting off-camera during filming of the TV performance scene in *A Hard Day's Night*. Paul doesn't look too impressed. Ringo would stick to playing the drums.

John, meanwhile, looks out from the wings of London's (now-demolished) Scala Theatre, perhaps trying to catch a glimpse of the audience. What he couldn't have known, however, was that this included a future star in the making, for, among the 350 fans who were paid union rate to sob and scream their lungs out, there was a 13-year-old actor who would one day achieve international fame in his own right. The kid's name? Phil Collins.

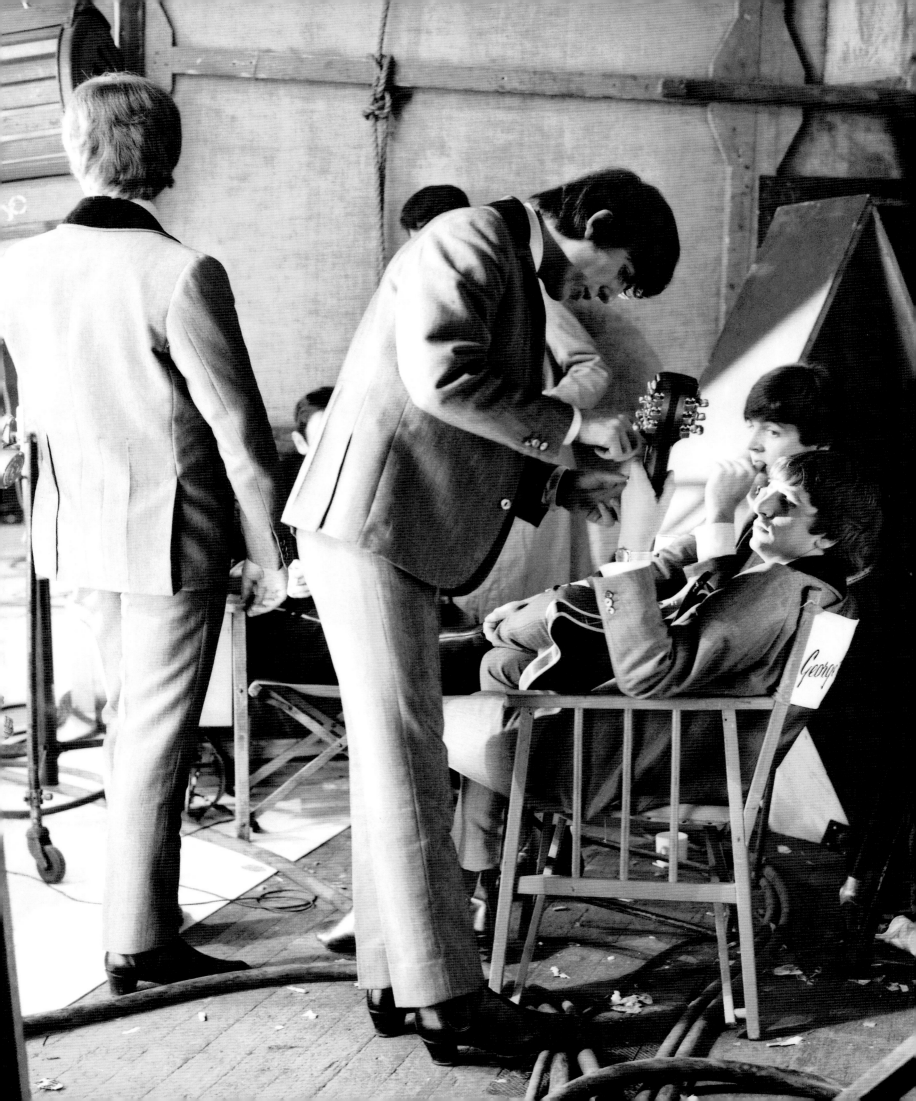

THEY sobbed, they screamed, they sighed, they smiled, they cheered, they stuffed handkerchiefs in their mouths, they even wet themselves . . . and they were paid to do it! (Well, perhaps not wet themselves, but some girls just lost all control.) That's why, before John and Paul wrote the song 'A Hard Day's Night', one of the working titles for the movie had been 'Beatlemania'.

The manic teenagers inside the Scala Theatre on March 31, 1964 hardly had to be coached or motivated when asked to go gaga over their idols, and they certainly weren't in need of the £7 10s (£7.50) fee that they each received. As you can see from this photo, the young thespians were able to emote right on cue, and while the female contingent comprised the vast majority of the audience there were also quite a few boys around to help rally things along. Such was The Beatles' widespread appeal even among the teenyboppers.

The blonde girl at center, with her hand up to her throat and a look of awestruck desperation on her face, can be clearly seen in the finished film as well as in the movie's publicity trailer, blubbering her guts out and moaning, "Jawj". (That's "George" with a heavy London accent — You can't hear her, but my lip-reading abilities are infallible.)

66

P AUL checks out the transistor radio, probably to find out what he and his colleagues have either said or done during the past 24 hours. By early 1964 not only were The Beatles' songs being broadcast all over the airwaves, but so were reports about their every move, Indeed, there was always so much speculation that the four main men themselves would have to catch up with the latest radio, television, newspaper and magazine items in order to learn what they were supposedly thinking or doing.

After all, wasn't Paul about to marry his girlfriend, actress Jane Asher? And what about those rumors that The Beatles were on the verge of splitting up? Issues such as these were clearly far more important than trivial political conflicts like that taking place in Vietnam, and so the Fab Four just had to keep in touch with the news.

"SPEAK oop, loov, I can't 'ear ya!" John Lennon, always the most caustic and quick-witted of The Beatles, didn't suffer fools gladly, and a devastating put-down would be his near-inevitable response to a simple-minded question from an unwitting reporter. Here are some samples:

Q: How does it feel, putting on the whole world?

John: How does it feel to be put on?

Q: Do you wear wigs?

John: If we do they must be the only ones with real dandruff.

Q: How do you account for your phenomenal success?

John: If we knew, we would form another group and be managers.

THE Beatles pose with the Rt. Hon. Sir Eric Harrison, Australian High Commissioner and no relation to the group's lead guitarist, at a cocktail party thrown in their honor on the evening of April 22, 1964. 700 people attended the function which was held at Australia House in the Strand, Central London, two months before John, Paul, George and Ringo set off on their tour Down Under. Running from June 12 to 30, this would take in venues in Adelaide, Melbourne, Sydney and Brisbane, as well as Wellington, Auckland, Dunedin and Christchurch in New Zealand.

PAUL and Ringo chomp into the Tasmanian apples that they and their fellow Beatles were asked to sample during the Australia House cocktail party. Other delights included hampers containing Australian champagne, canned pears, peaches and apricots, not to mention a set of kangaroo badges that they no doubt wore with pride.

The Australasian tour would gross more than £200,000, attract nearly 200,000 concertgoers and produce scenes of Beatlemania that were unrivaled anywhere else, including the U.S. Around 250,000 people congregated in the streets outside the band's hotel in Melbourne, and there were 300,000 on hand in Adelaide to see the Fab Four make a royal-style balcony appearance, during which John led his colleagues in greeting the masses with Nazi salutes, holding black combs above their top lips as a parody of Adolf Hitler's toothbrush moustache.

P AUL, John, George . . . and Jimmy? On the morning of June 3, 1964, a day before The Beatles' embarked on a tour of Denmark, The Netherlands and Hong Kong, Ringo collapsed during a group photo session, suffering from the effects of tonsilitis and pharyngitis. George in particular wanted to cancel the tour, but he was persuaded otherwise by Brian Epstein and producer George Martin. Consequently, later that morning Jimmy Nicol, a 24-year-old session drummer and leader of a band named The Shubdubs, received a telephone call summoning him to EMI's Abbey Road studios. That afternoon he rehearsed half a dozen numbers with his new/temporary colleagues, went home, packed his bags, and the following day they were playing on-stage together in Copenhagen.

Clearly, Jimmy had been chosen because, in addition to being familiar with Beatles material, he was sufficiently unknown to avoid press speculation about him being a permanent replacement for Ringo. So it was that, after enjoying instant superstardom performing with the world's greatest showbiz phenomenon in Denmark, the Netherlands, Hong Kong and Adelaide, Australia, Jimmy Nicol returned to immediate obscurity once Ringo rejoined his bandmates in Melbourne on June 14. He had earned £500 plus expenses and received a gold wrist-watch inscribed, "From The Beatles and Brian Epstein to Jimmy — with appreciation and gratitude." The following year he would declare bankruptcy, asserting that a falling-out with Epstein had led to him being blacklisted in the business. In 1995 his son, Howie, would be the sound recordist on the Beatles Anthology documentary series.

'I'M Flying' — That was the name of the aerial ballet sketch which Paul, John, George and Ringo participated in during the first half of *The Night Of A Hundred Stars*, a special midnight revue that took place at the London Palladium on July 23, 1964.

The Beatles illustrated their willingness to enter into the spirit of things by agreeing to be suspended by high wires that were attached to body braces. Fortunately none of their singing voices were affected as a result, because, as representatives of "pop music", they then had to perform a brief musical set during the second half of the show.

STAGED in aid of the Combined Theatrical Charities Appeals Council, *The Night Of A Hundred Stars* featured legends such as Sir Laurence Olivier and Judy Garland among its, er, stellar cast.

Here Paul, John and George pick up a few acting tips from Larry during rehearsals, while Ringo, riding high on the plaudits that he had recently received from film critics for his bravura performance in *A Hard Day's Night*, is distracted by other goings-on at the London Palladium.

${\rm T}$HE woman talking to John during rehearsals for *The Night Of A Hundred Stars* is Millicent Martin. A native of Romford, England, the then-30-year-old singer-actress had gained widespread popularity during the early Sixties for her weekly TV appearances on *That Was The Week That Was* (otherwise known as *TW3*), the satirical British revue hosted by David Frost and co-starring such luminaries as Roy Kinnear, Bernard Levin, Willie Rushton, Kenneth Cope and Lance Percival. After headlining in Anthony Newley and Leslie Bricusse's hit musical, *Stop the World, I Want to Get Off*, Martin starred in the short-lived 1971 TV sitcom, *From A Bird's Eye View*.

A dark-haired beauty with a Yorkshire Terrier catches the eyes of James McCartney and son Paul in this frank 1964 photo. McCartney Sr., whose first name was passed on to his famous offspring (and said offspring's own son), had played the piano in a ragtime outfit named Jim Mac's Band during his late teens and early twenties, and when Paul had found solace in music after his mother Mary's death, Jim had bought him a trumpet.

Quickly realizing that he couldn't play this and sing at the same time, Paul had dispensed with the brass instrument in favor of the guitar, and he would later also ignore his father's musical advice — When Jim first heard 'She Loves You' he insisted that the catchy refrain should be amended to the more grammatical "yes, yes, yes"!

James McCartney died on March 18, 1976.

THE all-conquering leaders of the 'British Invasion' — which saw America's pop-charts being swamped by acts such as Herman's Hermits, The Animals, The Dave Clark Five, Gerry and the Pacemakers, The Rolling Stones and The Kinks — pose in front of a beleaguered flag on the eve of their first US tour.

In *Billboard* magazine's 'Hot 100' singles listing for April 4, 1964, The Beatles had held the top five positions, in addition to numbers 31, 41, 46, 58, 65, 68 and 79 (a feat that no one has ever even come near matching). Now, following on from their triumphant *Ed Sullivan Show* appearances and concert debuts on American soil back in February, the Fab Four would slay all before them between August 19 and September 20.

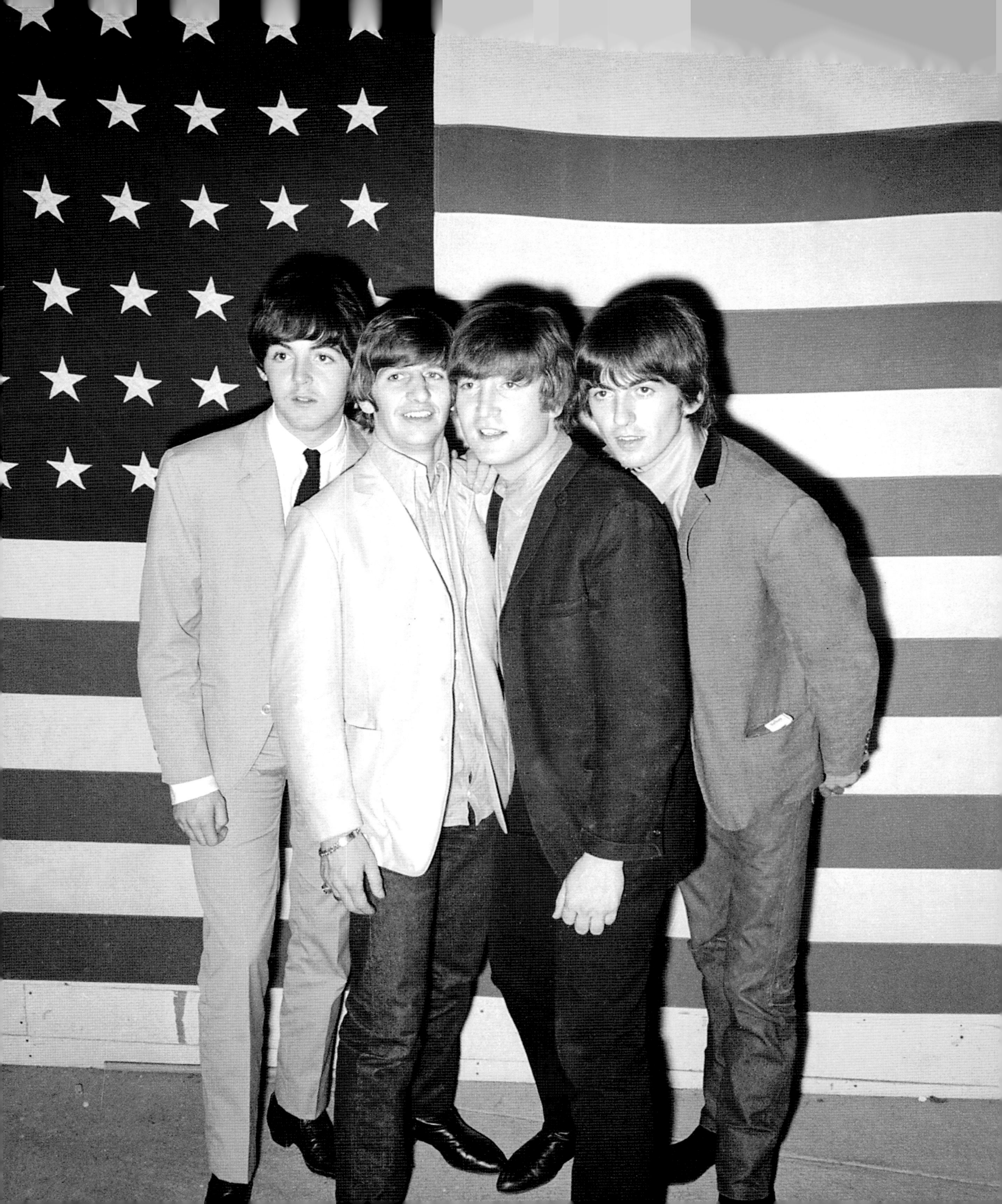

THEY went up the steps, they came down the steps — 1964 was a year like no other for The Beatles. Not only did they perform 32 shows in 24 cities within 33 days on their first jaunt around North America, but in addition to starring in their first film, recording two albums and making numerous TV and radio appearances, they also played in France, the Netherlands, Denmark, Hong Kong, Australia, New Zealand, Sweden and the UK. The British tour consisted of 54 shows in 25 cities within 33 days, and the band members then launched themselves into 'Another Beatles Christmas Show' at London's Hammersmith Odeon, comprising 38 shows over the course of 20 nights during December and January. Never again would they undertake this kind of schedule.

THE backroom boys — Following closely behind The Beatles as they descend from the plane in yet another American city are Brian Epstein, Derek Taylor and Neil Aspinall.

Neil — or 'Nell', as John used to call him — had attended the same Liverpool Institute high school as Paul and George, and as a close friend of The Beatles' early drummer, Pete Best, he would often help to drive the band to and from gigs around the city. When, soon after the group had attained a recording contract with EMI, Best was fired in August of 1962, Aspinall had considered turning his back on John, Paul and George, but they instead convinced him to quit his accountancy studies and become their full-time road manager. In 1968 he would subsequently be appointed Managing Director of their Apple Corps company, a position which he retains to this day.

AND here are our often-airborne heroes once again, except that this time around they are being followed down the steps by (at top, above John's head) their assistant, Malcolm Evans.

'Big Mal', as he was affectionately known, first met The Beatles when he was doing his evening job as a bouncer at Liverpool's Cavern Club. By day he was a post office engineer, but on August 11, 1963 he quit this steady career in order to relieve Neil Aspinall of heavy-duty work such as hauling the band's instruments and amplifiers from venue to venue. At the same time Mal served as their personal bodyguard, and during the ensuing years he would also contribute handclaps and assorted background instrumental parts on several Beatles recordings, before being appointed Assistant General Manager of their company, Apple, in 1968. After the group's breakup Mal produced and managed the Apple signing, Badfinger, and in 1973 he and George Harrison co-wrote 'You And Me (Babe)' for the album Ringo.

Mal Evans was shot dead by Los Angeles police on January 5, 1976, after they were called to his home when his girlfriend said he was threatening to commit suicide. In a state of mental confusion he allegedly turned his gun on the six officers and suffered the consequences.

92

AFTER kicking off 'The Beatles' First American Tour' at the Cow Palace in San Francisco on August 19, 1964, John, Paul, George and Ringo flew on immediately to the bright lights of Las Vegas, arriving there at 1 o'clock in the morning. They then performed two shows at the Convention Center, at 4 and 9pm, before a total of 16,000 delirious fans.

The group's repertoire for the tour amounted to the same 12 songs: 'Twist And Shout', 'You Can't Do That', 'All My Loving', 'She Loves You', 'Things We Said Today', 'Roll Over Beethoven', 'Can't Buy Me Love', 'If I Fell', 'I Want To Hold Your Hand', 'Boys', '*A Hard Day's Night*' and 'Long Tall Sally', the only exception being when 'She Loves You' would be dropped in favor of opening with 'I Saw Her Standing There' and closing with 'Twist And Shout'. However, at one of the Vegas gigs, the band also added 'Till There Was You'.

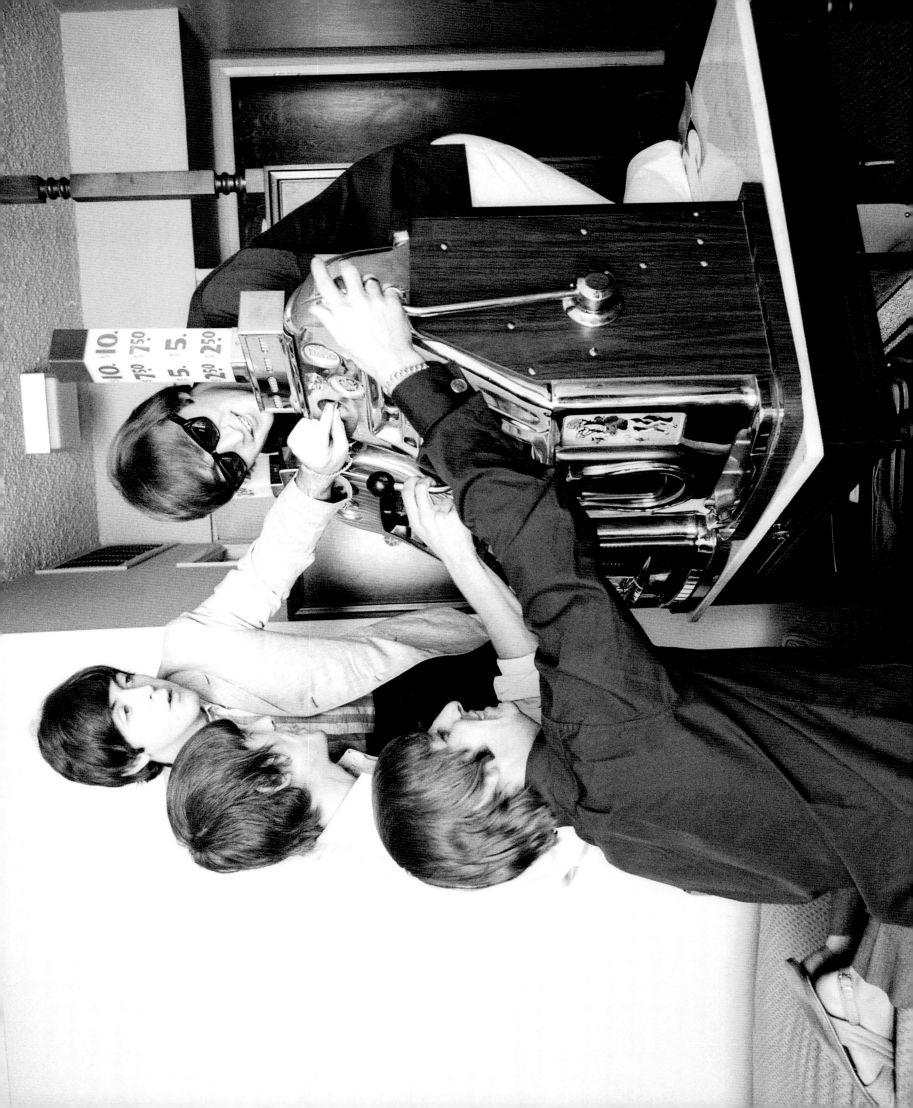

P AUL and Derek — Messrs. McCartney and Taylor fool around in The Beatles' suite prior to the band's two Las Vegas performances on August 20, 1964. Nevertheless, although Derek would be retained by The Beatles to serve as their press officer, writing publicity releases and album sleeve notes up to and including the Beatles Anthology record and video collections in 1995 and 1996, he and Paul were never close.

ALTHOUGH The Beatles didn't have the time or space to sit around the gambling tables of Las Vegas, they hit the financial jackpot on their first fully-fledged American tour and so did a number of enterprising businessmen.

Charles O. Finley, owner of the Kansas City Athletics baseball team, persuaded the band to add a date in his city on September 17 in return for a record-breaking $150,000. Thereafter, when The Beatles left Kansas, the manager of their hotel, The Muehlbach, sold the 16 sheets and 8 pillow cases from their suite to a pair of Chicago businessmen for $750. These two then cut the linen into three-inch squares, mounted it on card and sold it at $10 a square. Much the same fate had been accorded the towels with which The Beatles had wiped their faces after walking off stage at the Hollywood Bowl on August 23, not to mention their bath water and used shaving foam from a number of hotels. Meanwhile, in New York City, street traders were offering cans of 'Beatle Breath' to lucky passers-by.

"HAVE you heard the news?" Whatever Paul is talking about appears to be serious, and perhaps he has good reason for concern. Prior to the second of The Beatles' two shows at the Las Vegas Convention Center the venue's management received an anonymous bomb threat, and so when the group members took to the stage that evening it was in the knowledge that their lives were at considerable risk.

Not that this was the only time they had to deal with their own mortality during the 1964 U.S. tour. A previously-successful female astrologer predicted that The Beatles chartered airplane, which Brian Epstein had rented at a cost of $37,950.50, would crash en route from Philadelphia to Indianapolis on September 2 and that there would be no survivors. As it happens she wasn't all that far off the mark — In April of 1966 the same plane would indeed crash, killing more than 80 soldiers.

IN the full glare of the footlights — John handles the vocal, George concentrates on his guitar work and bassman Paul soaks up the atmosphere on an oversized stage in an outside American venue. And to think that just over a year before The Beatles had still been playing at places such as the Cavern Club in Liverpool, where a few hundred diehards would cram into a musty cellar and sit only a few feet in front of their heroes.

During the pre-fame years the audience could see and hear the band, the band could see and hear the audience, and the band members could also hear themselves, but once Beatlemania kicked into high gear it was a different story. Now the group had to perform at a safe — and therefore considerable — distance from the fans in venues that were usually large enough to cater to the huge demand for tickets, and given the level of female screaming, amplification equipment that would be laughable by today's standards and the fact that The Beatles had no foldback speakers with which to hear their own performance, it was a case of 'seen but not heard' all around.

Unbelievably, a set of 100 watt amplifiers, positioned at the back of the stage, were all that the band had in order to contend with the high-pitched audience wailing. No wonder, then, that on some occasions the Fab Four took to miming their songs. Nobody knew the difference.

102

"Can you blame him?" appears to be George's expression in response to Ringo's apparent proclamation. Nevertheless, unless Paul knows something that we don't, it's pretty likely that the cushion was made and donated by a Harrison fan.

Beatle People, as they soon started calling themselves, would often make things and send them to their idols, although sometimes their efforts to please did go a little too far. Witness the fans' reaction to a 1963 press bio which stated that George liked jelly babies (a British version of gummy bears). Thereafter, whenever The Beatles performed concerts in Britain and the U.S. during late-1963 and 1964 they would be quite literally pelted with jelly babies, gummy bears, jelly beans, you name it, and if they hit their unwitting targets they would hurt. Not too surprisingly, John commented that he and his colleagues would prefer it if the fans were to throw paper money at them.

WELL, somebody's got their attention. In every city that they visited on tour The Beatles had to hold the obligatory press conference and answer, for the most part, the same mind-numbing questions, day in, day out. At first John, Paul, George and Ringo excelled at the challenge of rattling off quick-fire responses to the reporters' inanities, but before long they ran out of patience with a daily diet that consisted of such probing queries as "What do you think of America?" and "What did you eat today?" Still, there were some amusing exchanges...

Q: Does all the adulation from teenage girls affect you?

John: When I feel my head start to swell, I look at Ringo and know perfectly well we're not supermen.

Q: Do teenagers scream at you because they are, in effect, revolting against their parents?

Paul: They've been revolting for years.

Q: What's your reaction to a Seattle psychiatrist's opinion that you are a menace?

George: Psychiatrists are a menace.

Q: Sorry to interrupt you while you are eating, but what do you think you will be doing in five years time when all this is over?

Ringo: Still eating.

AUGUST 24, 1964: Having performed at the legendary Hollywood Bowl the previous evening, George, John, Ringo and Paul play host at a Hollywood party attended by fans and celebrities alike. At the extreme right, actor Edward G. Robinson greets Paul, while in the foreground the pearl-laden woman sporting the subtle hat is gossip columnist Hedda Hopper. Standing just behind Paul on either side are Neil Aspinall (in dark glasses) and Derek Taylor, while the man looking towards the left behind John is assistant Mal Evans.

The seemingly endless cycle of meeting dignitaries and holding babies soon became yet another tiring facet of The Beatles' concert tours.

CLOWNING around during a day off in Bel Air, August 25, 1964. Following their meet 'n' greet Hollywood party, The Beatles spent some time relaxing at the private house which they had rented. Then, during the evening, Paul, George and Ringo visited actor Burt Lancaster to watch a private screening of Peter Sellers' latest film, *A Shot in the Dark*, while John stayed home to play the genial host to Jayne Mansfield, Bobby Darin and Sandra Dee. It could have been a million miles away from Liverpool...

WITH a look like that, what can she be thinking? Diana Vero, a secretary to Brian Epstein in the London offices of his management company, NEMS Enterprises, goes through some press clippings with Paul and George during a break in Bel Air.

Vero had first met The Beatles in 1963 while they were taping an appearance on the British television show, *Thank Your Lucky Stars*, and within a year she was working as Epstein's secretary and traveling to America as part of the Fab Four's entourage. She also typed her boss's autobiography, *A Cellarful Of Noise*, while Derek Taylor dictated, and in 1965 she moved to Los Angeles.

SOME people will do anything to attract attention — Ringo threatens to end it all during The Beatles' day off in Bel Air... and just when everything appeared to have been going so nicely for him.

Two years before, in August of 1962, the diminutive drummer had been playing a summer season with his band, Rory Storm and the Hurricanes, at Butlin's holiday camp in Skegness. Then, on the morning of the 15th, a phone call from Brian Epstein had led to him joining forces with John, Paul and George in return for a weekly wage of £25. Three days later he made his debut as a Beatle at a Horticultural Society dance in Chester, and after that things just went from strength to strength.

Now here he was, earning a lot more than £25 a week...

As it happens, the gun and holster tied in with Ringo's long-standing love of cowboy movies and country & western music. Among his boyhood heroes were Gene Autry, Hank Williams and Buck Owens, and in October of 1961, bored with the routine of playing with Rory Storm and the Hurricanes, he actually wrote to the Chamber of Commerce in Houston, Texas, with a view to emigrating there. Filling out the necessary forms and cutting through the bureaucratic red tape proved to be a daunting task, however, and so Ringo remained in Liverpool until fate intervened.

"IF you don't know how to finish the job, let me show you . . . "
George gives Ringo some friendly advice in the art of pulling the trigger.

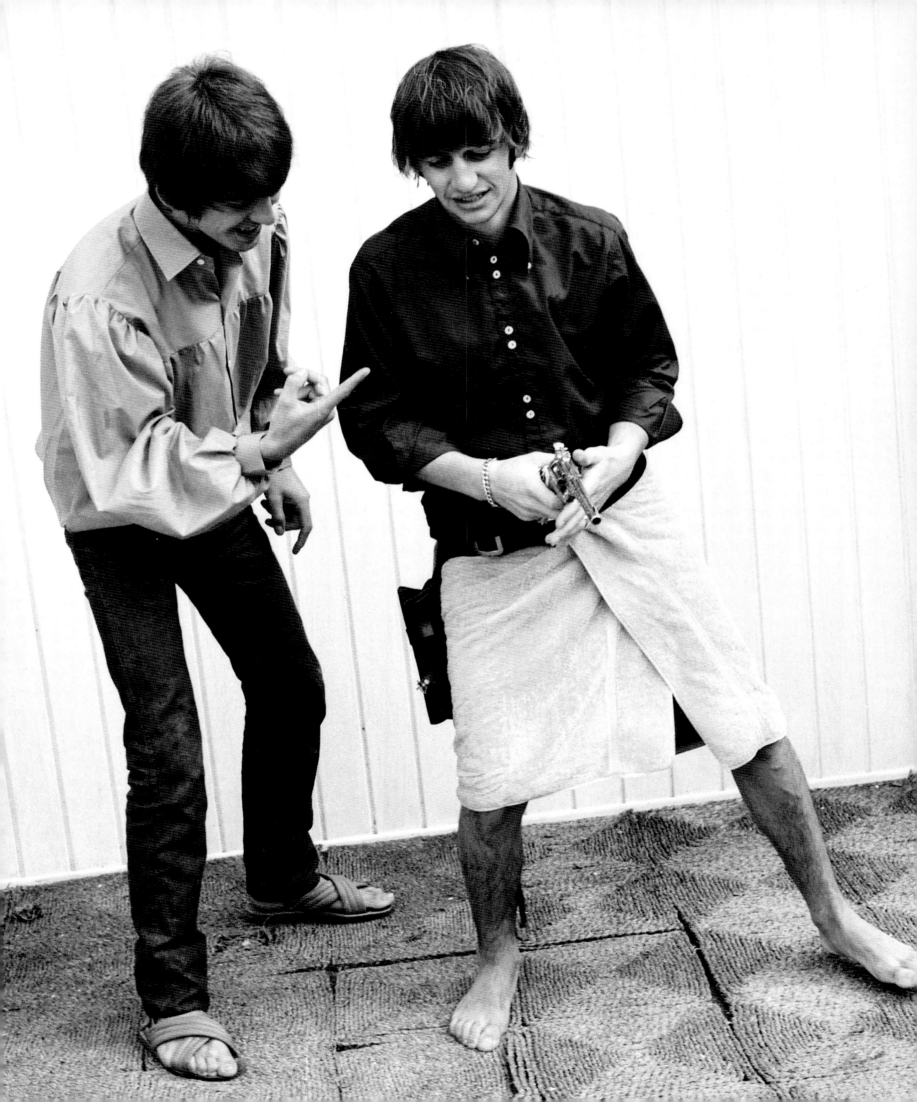

PAUL chats with a fan while catching up on the latest Beatles-related headlines at a press conference in Cincinnati, Ohio on August 27, 1964. Neil Aspinall is at top left.

When asked by a reporter at the conference what the group planned to do when all of the fan worship eventually died down, John replied, "Count the money." To another who asked for their opinions on a psychiatrist who had compared the hysteria at Beatles concerts to that at Hitler's Nazi rallies, the Lennon response was even more curt: "Tell him to shut up. He's off his head." And all four Fabs admitted to the fact that the show which took place in their hotel room after each concert was probably the one to see — Apparently they would often "whoop it up" until 4 or 5 in the morning.

Still, while The Beatles were performing before 14,000 people at the Cincinnati Gardens, thieves broke into their dressing room and stole cash together with other personal belongings.

THE getaway — Planning The Beatles' entrance and departure to and from an airport, hotel or concert venue was virtually a military-style procedure during the Beatlemania years of 1963 to 1966. Many of their adoring fans simply wanted to express their love for the group, others perhaps wanted a part of them, but either way there was a serious and on-going risk to life and limb for John, Paul, George and Ringo.

Not that they saw much — or perhaps anything — of the cities that they 'visited' during a tour. Normally the routine went like this: After arriving at the airport they would be ushered straight into the obligatory press conference, and from there they would be driven to their hotel, where they would meet the usual assortment of dignitaries but otherwise remain imprisoned in their suite until it was time for the concert. At that point they would be driven to the venue, they would perform a half-hour show, and then they would crowd into the back of a limo or armored car and head straight for the airport, en route to their next destination.

Life on the road wasn't nearly as exciting as the public perceived it to be.

GEORGE chats on the phone and glances at the local Beatles-infested newspaper, while a young lovely reclines on his bed during a meet-the-press session in the group's hotel suite. She could afford to look contented; others would have literally killed for this opportunity.

At the band's hotel in Dallas on September 18 a chambermaid was kidnapped at knifepoint by an over-zealous fan and urged to reveal which suite The Beatles were staying in. She refused and the girl was eventually dragged away. Meanwhile, several other frenzied females were discovered hiding in an air-conditioning shaft within the same hotel! No wonder the Fab Four were feeling the heat.

"I'M a Beatle stewardess. Fly me!" Of the 22,621 miles that John, Paul, George and Ringo traveled during their August 18–September 21, 1964 American trip, 22,441 of these were in the air. Just imagine all of that in-flight food!

George would later liken their existence to that of monkeys in a zoo, for while the touring miles declined after 1964 the personal hazards certainly didn't. Witness an incident which took place on August 19, 1965, when The Beatles' plane touched down in Houston, Texas. It was 2 o'clock in the morning, yet there were still 5,000 rabid fans waiting to catch a glimpse of their idols. As the plane taxied to a halt the kids broke through police cordons and surrounded the carrier, even climbing on top of the wings to peer through the windows. On the inside the trapped passengers were petrified, yet 40 minutes passed before they could make their escape by jumping into a service truck from a nine-foot-high emergency exit at the back of the plane.

And to think; Lloyd's of London had dared to insure The Beatles against personal injury to the collective tune of $22 million.

BRIAN Epstein ushers his famous charges out of the airport lounge and into full view of the waiting crowds — Airport receptions were a large part of what Beatlemania was all about, yet when the first of these took place on October 31, 1963, the men at the center of the fuss were taken totally by surprise. Touching down at London's Heathrow on their return from a tour of Sweden, John, Paul, George and Ringo could see hundreds of screaming fans standing atop the Queen's Building in the pouring rain while journalists and photographers waited on the ground. They naturally assumed that a high-powered dignitary was arriving. They were wrong.

Whenever The Beatles departed from or returned to Heathrow during 1964 and 1965 thousands of Beatlemaniacs would be there to greet them, and the airport would even play the band's music over its public address system. Similar scenes took place wherever the Fab Four flew to around the world, and although the crowds began to diminish slightly in 1966 they only stopped turning up once The Beatles had quit the road for good.

RINGO holds up his broken neck-chain and sports a ripped shirt after his latest mauling at the hands of some over-eager fans. Still, this was all part and parcel of being one of the four most famous men on Earth during the mid-Sixties.

On August 21, 1964, a girl fell from an overhead beam and landed at Ringo's feet just as the band was leaving the stage of the Seattle Coliseum. Then, on September 15, more than 200 Beatlemaniacs charged the stage of Cleveland's Public Auditorium and held up the show, before mounted police trapped them all in a large net.

What this kind of behavior had to do with the music was anyone's guess.

CHAOS in Colorado — Bedlam ensues on The Beatles arrival in Denver on 26 August, 1964, yet this was one of the few places which the group visited on its first U.S. tour where they didn't manage to sell out a fairly average-sized concert venue.

Only 7,000 fans turned up to see John, Paul, George and Ringo performing in the natural outdoors setting of the Red Rocks Amphitheatre, meaning that another 2,000 tickets remained unsold. As to the reason, the only one that anyone could come up with pointed to the venue's location, 20 miles outside of the city where there was no public transportation. The Beatles never returned to Colorado.

GEORGE draws on a ciggie and reads all about how to cover up ugly veins. After all, what else was there to do while waiting in the hotel suite before showtime?

In San Francisco on August 18, on the first leg of their 1964 U.S. tour, The Beatles were ensconced on the 15th floor of the Hilton Hotel. Armed policemen and security guards were buzzing all over the place, yet none of them reacted when a woman was beaten unconscious and robbed nine floors below. They simply assumed that the screams were those of yet another out-of-control fan!

Now these young women all appear to be behaving with decorum as they come face to face with their idols, backstage just prior to the start of a concert. Unfortunately, not all of The Beatles' audience encounters were quite so pleasant.

John would later describe how after many of their shows they would be greeted by people with terrible physical ailments and deformities, who would inevitably try to touch one or more of the Fab Four in the vain hope of being healed by their 'magic touch'. The Beatles themselves were horrified by this, but some people were quickly losing sight of them as normal human beings.

B RIAN Epstein has a word with his four favorite clients as they sit in their limo during a thankfully peaceful stop-off on the road.

The manager of his parents' Liverpool city center record store when he formally began managing The Beatles at the start of 1962, Brian had not only delivered on his promise to secure them a recording contract but, by 1964, had also helped them attain something that only he alone had ever considered possible; they were now even bigger than Elvis Presley. It had been quite a trip in little over two years, from scruffy, leather-clad no-hopers to world-conquering superstars, and without Brian's vision, belief and dedication it's fairly likely that it would never have taken place.

Although he quickly assembled an entire stable of artists — including Gerry and the Pacemakers, Billy J Kramer with the Dakotas, Cilla Black and The Fourmost — and would eventually become a theater-owner and all-round pop-impressario, Brian Epstein's main love was always The Beatles. Consequently, the group's decision to stop touring in 1966 would coincide with him losing his own sense of purpose and direction. Thereafter they would no longer rely nearly as much on his input and assistance, and it would be while feeling dejected about his future and despondent about his unhappy homosexual lifestyle that Brian would die of a drug overdose at the age of 32 on August 27, 1967.

"BYE-BYE... so long..." Another city, another show, and straight on to the next one before the sweat has even dried from their faces.

A half-hour performance was all that a Beatles concert amounted to, yet, given all of the rushing around and the frenzied atmosphere that they constantly found themselves in, John, Paul, George and Ringo were usually frazzled by the time that they ran off-stage. Still, the fans did get a little more for their money — Support acts on 'The Beatles' First American Tour' were The Bill Black Combo, The Exciters, The Righteous Brothers and Jackie DeShannon

DURING the Beatlemania years Ringo Starr was the most popular member of the Fab Four in the United States, and if any proof of this was needed it became clear to one and all when the 24-year-old drummer entered London's University College Hospital on December 1, 1964 in order to have his tonsils removed.

It's not often that the patient first has to hold a press conference prior to this standard procedure, yet that's exactly what Ringo did. Nevertheless, while the basic idea was to temper media interest, the news reporters — especially those Stateside — simply picked up the ball and ran with it. Ringo underwent his tonsillectomy on December 2, and in America there were hourly radio bulletins informing concerned listeners about his progress.

There was no need for panic. When Ringo sang 'Act Naturally' on The Beatles' next album it was clear that his voice was still in fine fettle.

BETWEEN December 24, 1964 and January 16, 1965 the Fab Four appeared at London's Hammersmith Odeon in 'Another Beatles Christmas Show', a music-and-comedy package which ran for 38 performances over the course of 20 nights.

   After the second show of the evening on Friday, January 8, John, Paul and Ringo popped around the corner to take in a private viewing of the annual Boat Show at the Earl's Court Exhibition Building, and needless to say, the press were on hand to capture all of the fun.

"WHICH way to the front?" — Arriving at Earl's Court after the Boat Show's 9.00 pm public closing time, The Beatles (without George, who was otherwise engaged) paddled around a man-made lake in a rubber dinghy, and then made their way upstairs and headed straight for the mini powerboat race stand. There John, Paul and Ringo each steered a radio-controlled, 12-inch replica around a scaled-down model of the Isle of Wight, and they had such a good time that they didn't leave until after midnight.

SERIOUS protection appears to be a somber matter as a pair of bobbies do their duty, watching over Britain's four most valuable exports.

The police were called upon constantly when Beatlemania was at its height, holding back fans at concert venues, film premieres and any other locations where The Beatles were making public appearances. Nevertheless, towards the tail end of 1963 one loose-tongued Labour Member of Parliament had actually stood up in the House of Commons and suggested that all police protection for the group should be withdrawn! As far as he was concerned it was an unnecessary expense, even though he also very nearly needed police protection once his comment had reached the ears of irate fans.

THE man in black — An atmospheric portrait of The Beatles' 22-year-old lead guitarist, post-fame but pre-spiritual enlightenment.

Following the removal of a tumor in 1998, George would give an interview to British weekly newspaper *The News of the World* in which he would discuss how he smoked cigarettes when he was younger, and then gave them up only to resume the habit in recent years.

**K**EEPING those moptops dry while taking a fully-clothed plunge in the pool of the Nassau Beach Hotel, located in the West Bay area of New Providence in the Bahamas, February 23, 1965. This was for the first joint scene to be filmed on The Beatles' second, as-yet-untitled movie, *Help!*

Filming took place in the British crown colony until March 9, and this wasn't only to add glamour to the finished product. The Bahamas had recently been established as a tax haven for 'the boys', and so their financial adviser, Dr. Walter Strach, who was obliged to live there, suggested that it would be wise to film on the island as a goodwill gesture. Given the British weather at that time of year The Beatles weren't about to object, and neither would producer Walter Shenson or director Richard Lester — They were told that filming would commence in the Bahamas, and that was that.

ALL four Beatles emerge from the pool of the Nassau Beach Hotel, and they don't look nearly as enthralled with the whole experience as do the assorted sightseers.

The Fab Four actually stayed at the Balmoral Club near Cable Beach while filming in the West Indies, yet wherever they went on the 21-mile-long island there were not only plenty of local onlookers but also numerous foreign journalists and photographers on assignment. Consequently, a number of radio, newspaper and magazine interviews took place here.

"THERE must be easier ways to make a living!" Paul and a female member of the film crew are evidently amused by the spectacle of John being doused in cold water for a pick-up shot of the swimming pool scene at the Nassau Bay Hotel.

"There's no question of The Beatles playing anything but The Beatles," said producer Walter Shenson at the time. "The pop market is a teenage market and, by its standards, the boys have had a fantastically long run, and nobody can expect it to go on forever. But I've no doubt they can establish themselves as great screen personalities."

HE who laughs first doesn't always laugh last — Now it's Paul's turn to receive the hydro-shock treatment.

Filmed in color in glamorous locales whereas *A Hard Day's Night* had been shot in black-and-white amid more gritty-looking London settings, *Help!* — as it would eventually be titled — placed 'the boys' in a comic-strip-type fantasy. As a result the cameraman and the director were the real stars, and John and Paul would later state that they felt like guests in their own movie.

158

WOULD you do this to a Beatle? While Ringo appears to have escaped without punishment, George manfully takes his drenching at the hands of a suitably expressionless crew member. After all, some misplaced laughter might very well end in tears.

The publicity trailer for *Help!* would include a few seconds of a scene featuring George trapped inside a glass bubble, yet this would be one of several segments to be excised from the finished movie. So, how and why was it in the trailer? Well, in years past, movie studios would have special departments to deal with promotional film material, and they would receive all footage before the actual editing process took place. It therefore wasn't uncommon for a few seconds of a soon-to-be-cut scene to find their way into the trailer.

160

F EBRUARY 24, 1965: Paul, Ringo, George and John display their peddling skills as they cycle along Interfield Road, not far from the New Providence airport. They would also shoot some additional takes here the following day.

As conceived by writer Marc Behm, the group's second film had originally been intended as a vehicle for Peter Sellers. Behm's previous screen credits had included the Audrey Hepburn/Cary Grant picture, *Charade*, but director Dick Lester didn't feel that his latest script was perfectly matched to the Fab Four. He therefore brought in Charles Wood, who had just fashioned the script for Lester's comedy *The Knack*, to make the necessary revisions. The results went under the unimaginative working title of 'Beatles 2'.

BARE-CHESTED director Richard Lester is

among the onlookers as John cycles around on Interfield Road. While a production budget of £500,000 had been set aside by United Artists for the Fab Four's second big-screen venture — roughly twice the amount that had been allotted to *A Hard Day's Night* — Lester's own fee had risen to around £15,000, so he had good reason to appear happy.

American-born but British-based, Dick Lester had directed two pictures that The Beatles were familiar with prior to them first collaborating on *A Hard Day's Night*. One of these was *The Running, Jumping And Standing Still Film*, a zany Peter Sellers comedy short that John, Paul, George and Ringo had long been fans of, while the other was the cheapie pop vehicle, *It's Trad Trad*, which had featured a performance by their rock hero, Gene Vincent, whom they had supported on a concert bill back in Liverpool during the early-Sixties.

RINGO takes his turn at attracting the attention of bikini-clad sightseers along Interfield Road. Given his aforementioned popularity among fans, and the plaudits that he had earned from critics for his solo scene in *A Hard Day's Night*, The Beatles' drummer was really assigned the central role in the band's new movie, which focussed on the bungled attempts by an Eastern religious sect to remove a sacred ring from his finger.

The on-screen results would be mildly amusing, but not nearly as credible as those of the previous black-and-white outing.

ANY chance of a quick endorsement? Whether or not he's aware of it, Paul is doing more than just pose with a young admirer, and the Nassau Bicycle Company is clearly not the only beneficiary.

During their halcyon years The Beatles were often approached by huge corporations or enterprising advertising agencies to lend their name to any number of products, but in most cases they steadfastly refused, quite rightly feeling that this would compromise their artistic integrity among music critics and fans alike. Still, there was the odd commodity, such as Colgate's 'Beatle-Beatle Personality [bubble] Bath' ("Yeah! Yeah! Yeah! It's New! It's Wild! It's Pink Mild!") which somehow made its way onto supermarket shelves.

LAPPING up the good life — The Beatles worked on both weekends while they were in the Bahamas, and on Saturday, February 27 they shot several sequences on Balmoral Island, including that in which they mimed to the Lennon-McCartney composition, 'Another Girl'.

"We just write songs and they are fitted into the film," Paul explained at the time. "We're not like other songwriters who get suggestions from certain lines in a script. Often we write tunes first without having a title. We'll get that later."

170

JOHN takes a break from filming by quite literally putting his feet up in the back seat of The Beatles' limo. He would later refer to this time as his 'fat Elvis' period.

"The whole Beatle thing was beyond comprehension," he would tell *Playboy* magazine in 1980. "I was eating and drinking like a pig and I was fat as a pig, dissatisfied with myself, and subconsciously I was crying for help. I think everything comes out in the songs . . . When *Help!* came out I was actually crying out for help . . . it was my fat Elvis period. You see the movie: He — I — is very fat, very insecure, and he's completely lost himself. And I am singing about when I was so much younger and all the rest, looking back at how easy it was."

O KAY, who's the culprit? — John, Ringo and Paul, together with co-star Eleanor Bron, point the finger of suspicion at George, although quite what he's done to deserve this is anyone's guess.

Bron, who portrayed Ahme, a villainess-turned-ally, in The Beatles' second movie, was by coincidence the daughter of a music publisher who had once employed the group's own music publisher, Dick James.

THE Babyface

THE Quiet One

THE Sad-Eyed Clown

MARCH

MARCH 13, 1965: Two days after returning to London from the Bahamas, The Beatles, together with Ringo's wife Maureen and John's spouse Cynthia, are cheered off by thousands of screaming fans before catching the 11.00 am flight from Heathrow to Salzburg in Austria, for further location filming. There they would be greeted by a 4,000-strong crowd.

Ringo and Maureen had married the previous month at Caxton Hall in London, with John and George among the guests while Paul was on holiday in Tunisia. Here Macca gives what may well be among the first of his many thumbs-up to the cameras — Down the years this has become something of a trademark gesture.

THROUGHOUT their Austrian stay, which lasted until March 22, The Beatles were based at the Hotel Edelweiss in Obertauern, and it was in front of this establishment that shooting commenced on the 14th. The first scene to be shot was a 'toboggan rent' sequence that didn't make the movie's final cut, but which has nevertheless been captured in this elevated view of the overall setup.

Numerous scenes were edited out of the finished film, including one featuring comedian Frankie Howerd in the role of acting teacher Sam Ahab together with Wendy Richards as his pupil. Sadly, none of this footage still exists, the standard studio policy in years gone by having been to destroy it about a year after a film's release.

10 shillings per hour is an offer too good to refuse for our heroes, even if they're not prepared to splash out on more than one toboggan.

It was at around this time that the film took on the appellation of 'Eight Arms to Hold You', as suggested by Ringo in light of the fact that 'Beatles 2' wouldn't provide a very lyrical name for the obligatory Lennon-McCartney title song. Consequently, when Capitol issued the group's 'Ticket To Ride' single in the U.S. the record's label described it as being 'from the United Artists release "Eight Arms To Hold You",' yet by then (mid-April) UA, producer Walter Shenson, director Dick Lester and The Beatles themselves had all settled on *Help!* as the movie's title.

LOOKING debonair in his black cape and top hat, George points in the direction that he'll shortly be headed — It was on the set of Help! that he first picked up a sitar, and this in turn fueled his interest in not only Indian music but, subsequently, Eastern culture and religion.

Still, prior to the film going into production, the lead guitarist had expressed a desire for there to be no songs in the picture. "I don't like these films where everybody bursts into song for no reason and you have a full orchestra blasting out of nowhere," he'd said. "Yes, I'd prefer to make a film without any singing." Perhaps, yet as things turned out the Help! soundtrack featured seven new Beatles tracks, including George's own 'I Need You'.

M R. McCartney prepares himself for the slopes, before indulging in a spot of après-ski.

As the film company's insurance didn't cover any accidents that The Beatles might be involved in on the slopes, the stars of the movie were instructed just to stand in the stunning setting of the Austrian Alps and leave the downhill antics to a quartet of stunt-doubles; Cliff Diggins, Mick Dillon, Peter Cheevers and Joe Dunne. However, never ones to take orders from anyone, John, Paul, George and Ringo still made cursory attempts at skiing, and provided with this opportunity Dick Lester decided to keep the cameras rolling. The results ended up in the movie.

PAUL and Ringo keep an eye on the action, while the price of renting a toboggan appears to be falling by the hour.

The Beatles would all later reveal that, partly to relieve their boredom with the sluggish film-making process, they smoked pot while working on *Help!* and that as a result many scenes had to be shot time and time again because they kept fluffing their lines and laughing. Indeed, Ringo would later recall how a scene in which a bomb was due to explode at a curling rink required Paul and himself to run away. "Action!" was called and they ran on cue, but then when the director shouted "Cut!" they continued to run... and run, as far away as possible. All that they were interested in doing was hiding and lighting up another joint!

194

TOBOGGAN
HIRE

5/- PER HOUR

J̲ULY 29, 1965: Paul, Ringo, Maureen, John, Cynthia and George pose for the surrounding press photographers on their arrival at the London Pavilion cinema in Piccadilly Circus for the royal world charity premiere of *Help!*

As with the launch of *A Hard Day's Night* at the same venue 12 months before, the vast hordes of sightseers brought the local West End traffic to a virtual standstill, while after the screening The Beatles once again attended a private celebration party at the Dorchester Hotel.

Six and a half months pregnant at the time of the *Help!* premiere, Maureen would give birth to her and Ringo's first child at Queen Charlotte's Hospital in London on September 13, 1965. Named Zak by his father, their son would one day follow in Ringo's footsteps, drumming with him on tour as well as with The Who and Roger Daltrey. All this in spite of the elder Starr's insistence on the day of the birth that "I won't let Zak be a drummer!"

WHILE Brian Epstein (partly hidden by George) adjusts his bow, Ringo obliges with a quick autograph on his way in to the London Pavilion. Now, if the beneficiary of this gesture held onto the artifact and kept it in good condition, it could certainly be worth a tidy three-figure sum. A nice return on a zero investment, yet, given the abundance of such signatures, not nearly as much as the value that has been attached at auction to original, handwritten song lyrics. Topping the charts to date in this respect is 'Getting Better', a McCartney composition from The Beatles' landmark 1967 *Sgt. Pepper's Lonely Hearts Club Band* album, which a few years ago fetched no less than £161,000 ($230,000)!

MEETING the press in an English pub, 1965 — 'Liquid Apples' may have been the in-house delicacy of the day, but The Beatles' own Apple group of companies wouldn't be boasting too many liquid assets later in the decade.

A retail clothing division, an arts foundation, a film division, an electronics division and a music publishing division would all flounder amid an atmosphere of naive optimism on the part of the four main shareholders, and cynical opportunism on the part of those who succeeded in draining the company's resources. Only the Apple Records label turned in a profit, and that was basically due to a client roster that included Badfinger, James Taylor, Mary Hopkin, Billy Preston . . . and The Beatles.

THERE are smiles all around as a young female fan finally gets those invaluable signatures on her favorite album covers. Only George, who is apparently warning the photographer about a shady-looking character sitting just behind him, doesn't share in all of the fun and laughter.

Brian Epstein had originally proposed that, following The Beatles' 1965 tour of North America, they should undertake an autumn/winter tour of the UK, make a return appearance at the Royal Command Performance and commit themselves to a third series of Christmas shows. The Fab Four, however, were having none of it, and on August 2 there was an announcement that "The Beatles will not be undertaking a tour of Britain this year". Then, on September 1, there was another statement confirming that they would indeed tour, and, after all of the details were ironed out with promoter Arthur Howes, an extremely short, nine-date, eight-city itinerary was drawn up for December.

This would be The Beatles' last ever tour of their homeland. They were tired of the screams that inhibited their live performances and wanted to concentrate on work in the recording studio.

ON August 11, 1966, before setting off on their last-ever tour of the U.S.A. and Canada, Ringo, George, John and Paul check out the security operation at London's Heathrow Airport. At that moment, however, it was security overseas that they were really more concerned about.

A few weeks earlier The Beatles' five shows at the Nippon Budokan Hall in Tokyo, Japan, had provoked public demonstrations by those who considered the venue sacred and only suitable for martial arts. A 35,000-strong security force had to maintain order. Then, from Japan the group had flown straight to the Philippines and into even more trouble. In short, deception by the local concert promoter had led to false charges about The Beatles "snubbing" the First Lady, Imelda Marcos, by failing to attend a reception that she had thrown in their honor. (They had already declined the invitation.) As a result The Beatles had lost their share of the concert receipts and, amid numerous death threats, the security forces had withdrawn their protection, allowing the band members and their entourage to be punched and kicked by an unrestrained mob of 200 angry Filipinos prior to their airport departure.

Now The Beatles were on their way to America, where a storm had already erupted when a teen magazine misquoted some remarks that John had made to the London Evening Standard about the decline of mainstream religion. His comment that the Fab Four were "more popular than Jesus now" had somehow been transposed into them being "bigger than Jesus", and the result had been the banning of Beatles records on some US radio stations as well as the organization of public 'Beatle bonfires'. John subsequently apologized (!) but the tour was still marred by death threats and protests.

After 1966 The Beatles would never perform a proper concert ever again.

CERTIFIED COPY of an **ENTRY OF BIRTH**

Pursuant to the Births and **Deaths Registration Act 1953**

Registration District **Liverpool South**

1943. Birth in the Sub-district of **Wavertree** in the **County Borough of Liverpool.**

Columns:—	1	2	3	4	5	6	7	8	9	10*
No.	When and where born	Name, if any	Sex	Name, and surname of father	Name, surname and maiden surname of mother	Occupation of father	Signature, description and residence of informant	When registered	Signature of registrar	Name, if added after registration
357	Twenty Fifth February 1943 12 Arnold Grove	George Boy	Boy	Harold Hargreaves HARRISON	Louise HARRISON formerly FRENCH	Corporation Bus Driver	H.H. Harrison Father 12. Arnold Grove Liverpool 15	Twenty sixth February 1943	H. Thorne	

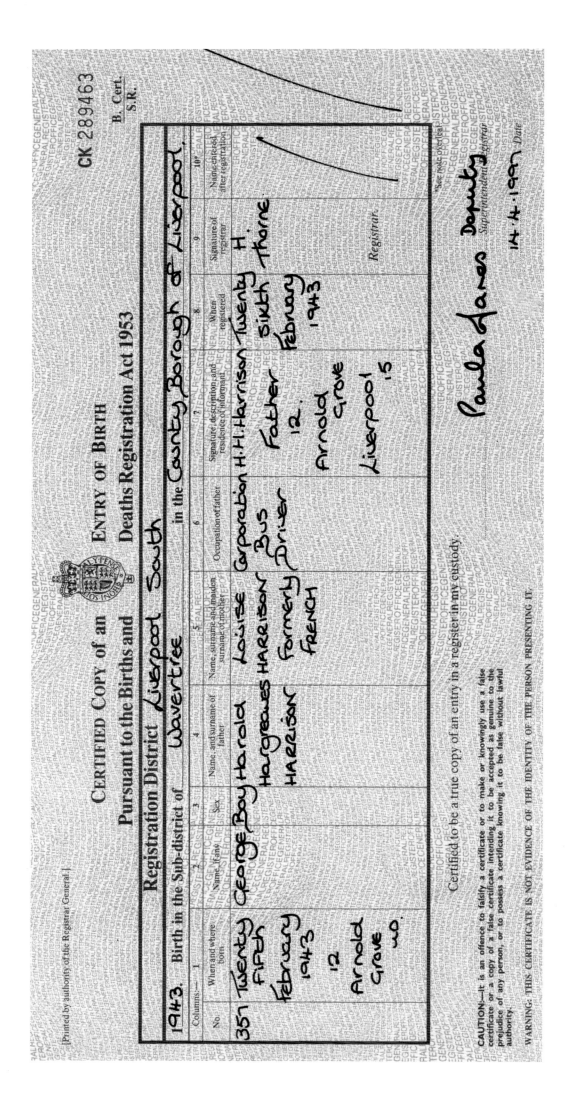

Certified to be a true copy of an entry in a register in my custody.

Paula James Superintendent Registrar

14.4.1997 Date

See note overleaf

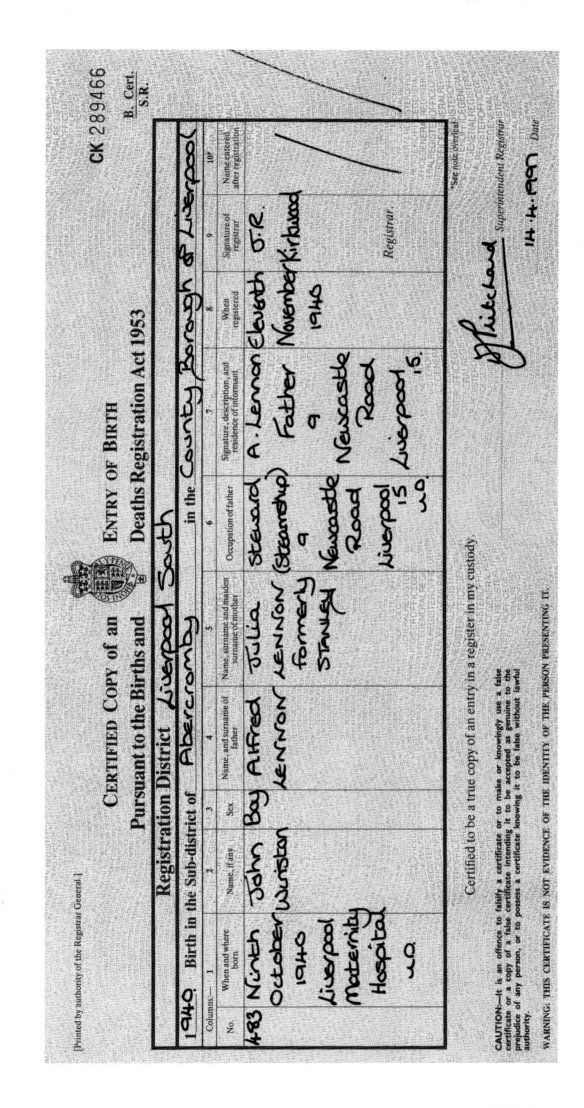

[Printed by authority of the Registrar General.]

CK 289466

B. Cert.
S.R.

CERTIFIED COPY of an ENTRY OF BIRTH

Pursuant to the Births and Deaths Registration Act 1953

Registration District **Liverpool South**

1940. Birth in the Sub-district of **Abercromby** in the **County Borough of Liverpool**

No.	1 When and where born	2 Name, if any	3 Sex	4 Name, and surname of father	5 Name, surname and maiden surname of mother	6 Occupation of father	7 Signature, description, and residence of informant	8 When registered	9 Signature of registrar	10* Name entered after registration
483	Ninth October 1940 Liverpool Maternity Hospital W.O.	John Winston	Boy	Alfred Lennon	Julia Lennon formerly Stanley	Steward (Steamship) 9 Newcastle Road Liverpool 15 W.O.	A. Lennon Elizabeth J.R. Father 9 Newcastle Road Liverpool 15.	Eleventh November 1940	Kirkwood J.R. Registrar.	

Certified to be a true copy of an entry in a register in my custody.

J. Whitelaw Superintendent Registrar

14.4.90 Date

CAUTION—It is an offence to falsify a certificate or to make or knowingly use a false certificate or a copy of a false certificate intending it to be accepted as genuine to the prejudice of any person, or to possess a certificate knowing it to be false without lawful authority.

WARNING: THIS CERTIFICATE IS NOT EVIDENCE OF THE IDENTITY OF THE PERSON PRESENTING IT.

*See note overleaf.

CK 289464

B. Cert.
S.R.

CERTIFIED COPY of an ENTRY OF BIRTH
Pursuant to the Births and Deaths Registration Act 1953

Registration District **Liverpool North**

1942. Birth in the Sub-district of **Walton Park** in the **County Borough of Liverpool**

No.	1. When and where born	2. Name, if any	3. Sex	4. Name, and surname of father	5. Name, surname and maiden surname of mother	6. Occupation of father	7. Signature, description, and residence of informant	8. When registered	9. Signature of registrar	10. Name entered after registration
240	Eighteenth June 1942 107 Rice Lane W.	James Paul	Boy	James McCartney	Mary Patricia McCartney formerly mohin.	Centre Lathe turner (aircraft factory of 10 Sunbury Road Liverpool W.	J. McCartney Father 10 Sunbury Road Liverpool	Fourteenth July 1942	W.S. Bailey	

Certified to be a true copy of an entry in a register in my custody.

Paula James   Deputy Superintendent Registrar

14.4.1997. Date

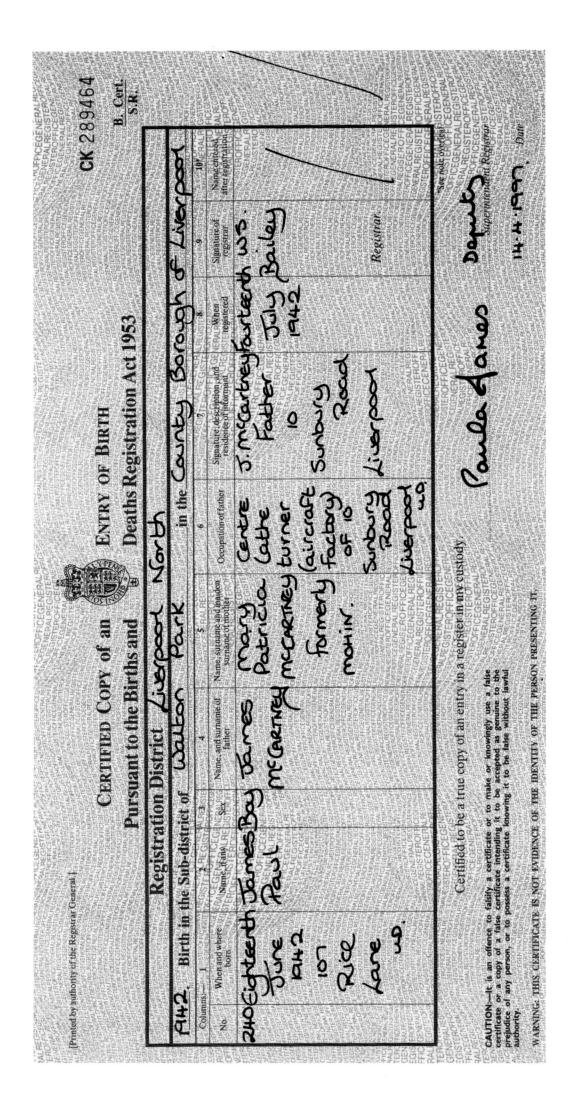

CK 289465

CERTIFIED COPY of an   ENTRY OF BIRTH

Pursuant to the Births and   Deaths Registration Act 1953

Registration District   Liverpool South

1940.   Birth in the Sub-district of   Toxteth Park   in the County Borough of Liverpool

No.	Columns:— 1 When and where born.	2 Name, if any	3 Sex	4 Name, and surname of father	5 Name, surname and maiden surname of mother	6 Occupation of father	7 Signature, description, and residence of informant	8 When registered	9 Signature of registrar	10* Name entered after registration
226	Seventh July 1940 9 Madryn Street w.o.	Richard	Boy	Richard STARKEY	Elsie STARKEY formerly GLEAVE	Confectioner (Cake maker)	E. Starkey M.J. mother 9 Madryn Street Liverpool 8.	First July 1940	Nichols	

Certified to be a true copy of an entry in a register in my custody.

Paula James Deputy   Superintendent Registrar

14.4.1977   Date

*See note overleaf.